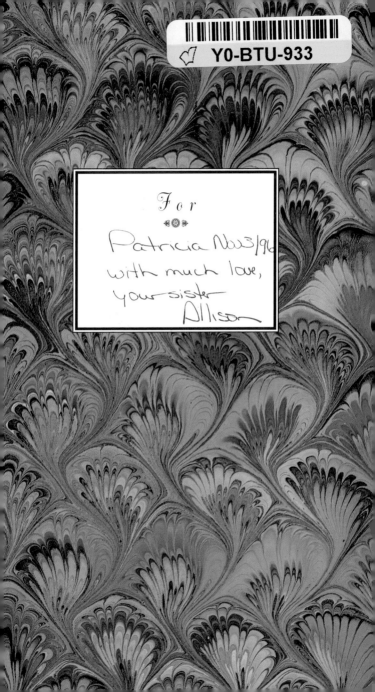

For

Patricia Nov 3/96
with much love,
your sister
Allison

My Sister

A Special Friend

Edited by Liesl Vazquez

❀❂❀

Design by Lesley Ehlers

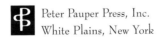

Peter Pauper Press, Inc.
White Plains, New York

❦ ❀ ❁ ❦ ❀ ❦

Photographs of Redgraves (cover) and
Pointer Sisters (p.36) courtesy of UPI/Bettmann Newsphotos.
Photographs of De Havilland/Fontaine (cover) and Talmadges
(p. 49) courtesy of the Bettmann Archive.
Photographs of Mandrells (cover), Bouviers (p. 53),
Minelli/Luft (p. 31), Gishes (p. 44),
Bennetts (p. 12), Gabors (p. 27),
Kennedys (p. 41), Meadows (p. 16), and
Queen Elizabeth II and Princess Margaret (p. 59) courtesy of
UPI/Bettmann. Photograph of Bouviers and mother (cover)
courtesy of FPG International Corp.

❦ ❀ ❁ ❦ ❀ ❦

Copyright © 1996
Peter Pauper Press, Inc.
202 Mamaroneck Avenue
White Plains, NY 10601
All rights reserved
ISBN 0-88088-491-6
Printed in Singapore.
7 6 5 4 3 2 1

My Sister

INTRODUCTION

Few relationships besides that of sisters yield such intense feelings of friendship, oneness, rivalry, and love. Truman Capote commented about the Bouvier sisters: *I think as a child Lee got away with murder. Her mother was much tougher on Jackie.*

Sisters cherish the special bonds of intimacy, traditions, and shared family history. Sisters can be our best friends, worst enemies, candid critics, unwavering supporters, or all of these, at different times throughout our lives. From childhood to adulthood, sisters act as our advisers and mentors, offering security, hope, and confidence.

Whether mirror images or complete opposites, sisters forever occupy a warm place in our hearts. So, turn the page and enjoy the witty, heartfelt, and revealing observations that renowned sisters have made about one another.

L. V.

A sister is both your mirror— and your opposite.

Elizabeth Fishel

◈ **O** ◈

I have got a new-born sister;
I was nigh the first that kissed her.
When the nursing-woman brought her
To papa, his infant daughter,
How papa's dear eyes did glisten!—
She will shortly be to christen;
And papa has made the offer,
I shall have the naming of her.

Now I wonder what would please her,—
Charlotte, Julia, or Louisa?
Ann and Mary, they're too common;
Joan's too formal for a woman;
Jane's a prettier name beside;
But we had a Jane that died.
They would say, if 't was Rebecca,
That she was a little Quaker.

◈ **O** ◈

Edith's pretty, but that looks
Better in old English books;
Ellen's left off long ago;
Blanche is out of fashion now.
None that I have named as yet
Are so good as Margaret.
Emily is neat and fine;
What do you think of Caroline?
How I'm puzzled and perplexed
What to choose or think of next!
I am in a little fever
Lest the name that I should give her
Should disgrace her or defame her;—
I will leave papa to name her.

Mary Lamb,
Choosing a Name

The Bennett Sisters

Marilyn was not a dumb blond. She was thoughtful and determined and a workaholic. She insisted on perfection from herself . . .

Berniece Baker Miracle,
sister of Marilyn Monroe

I adored Rosey. She was my first playmate, my first best friend. My mother told me that when Rosey started school, I was so devastated that I sat on the couch, looking out the window, waiting for her to return. There were days when I sat like that for hours.

Geraldine Barr,
about her sister, Roseanne

When my sister Claudia was born in 1947, the whole family constellation shifted. Suddenly there was "the baby." . . . Suddenly there was a baby nurse who wouldn't let me touch the baby because I had caught ringworm from my best friend's cat.

Erica Jong

OOOOOOOOOOOOOOOOOOOOOOOOOOOOOOOOOOOO

It can't have been easy for Jinny being my little sister. Then again, Mother was in her corner and bolstered her up between rounds. I was envious of their relationship, but I had Daddy, and that made things easier to bear.

Kitty Dukakis

❈ O ❈

From the very beginning it was clear she would be a source of excitement and challenge. There was healthy friction between us as she grew older, the type of competition that can only exist between two siblings cut from the same cloth.

Naomi Judd,
about her sister, Margaret

❈ O ❈

It seemed like wherever Eura was, that's where the seat of trouble was. She was always fighting trouble. It seemed that wherever she went, she was going to be hurt because she had so much tenderness in her—she's a darling sister.

Pearl Bailey

We acquire friends and we make enemies, but our sisters come with the territory.

Evelyn Loeb

The Meadows Sisters

I was a goody-goody; she was more defiant. . . .
But despite our differences and petty rivalries—
and apart from a period in my senior year when
we grew estranged—we were always the best of
friends.

Kathie Lee Gifford

⚛ **O** ⚛

Vaida and I shared a bed in the room with the
rose-colored lampshade. As the winter came, the
room was so cold that we had to wear sweaters
at night. She had a good red and green
Canadian cardigan. She would pull my back
close up to her, forming a lap for me. She was a
warming person. She had a coloratura voice and
was as beautiful as anyone I've ever seen.

Fay Wray

⚛ **O** ⚛

It is true that I was born in Iowa, but I can't
speak for my twin sister.

Abigail Van Buren,
Dear Abby

○○○○○○○○○○○○○○○○○○○○○○○○○○○○○○○○○○○○○○

Sixty-six years ago tonight I was hardly me. I was just a pink bundle snuggled in a blanket close to Mother. . . . The night before had been a disturbed one for everybody. Everything was quieted down tonight. The two-year-old Alice was deposed from her baby throne. The bigger girls were sprouting motherisms, all-over delighted with the new toy.

Emily Carr

☀ O ☀

I was always putting myself in my sister's place, adopting her credulousness, and even her memories, I saw, could be made mine. It was Isobel I imagined as the eternal heroine—never myself. I substituted her feelings for my own, and her face for any face described. Whatever the author's intentions, the heroine was my sister.

Mavis Gallant

 ☀ O ☀

ooooooooooooooooooooooooooooooooooooo

School parted us; we never found again
That childish world where our two spirits
    mingled
Like scents from varying roses that remain
One sweetness, nor can evermore be singled.

Yet the twin habit of that early time
Lingered for long about the heart and tongue:
We had been natives of one happy clime,
And its dear accent to our utterance clung.

Till the dire years whose awful name is Change
Had grasped our souls still yearning in divorce,
And pitiless shaped them in two forms
    that range
Two elements which sever their life's course.

But were another childhood-world my share,
I would be born a little sister there.

George Eliot,
School Parted Us

$\mathcal{W}$e've lived together most all of our lives, and probably know each other better than any two human beings on this Earth. After so long, we are in some ways like one person. She is my right arm.

Sarah Louise (Sadie) Delany,
about her sister, Bessie

Babe was always the glamor girl and I was always the crumbum except when I was away from her. Babe was a perfectionist. Compared to her I always felt insecure.

Betsy Whitney,
about her sister, Babe Paley

❋ **O** ❋

I was always wanting more from Susan. More time. More attention. More love. She always wanted me to bug off. . . . Despite my underlying resentment, my sister's presence always mattered. How happy I was to see her waiting outside school for me the day I got my first report card. How crushed I was the night my friend Ellen and I put on *The Pajama Game* for our families and Susan was out with her friends. . . . We are sisters. We will always be sisters. Our differences may never go away, but neither, for me, will our song.

Nancy Kelton

OOOOOOOOOOOOOOOOOOOOOOOOOOOOOOOOOOOOO

How could I be jealous of her? Everything she has she shares with me. I had a life-threatening illness just about the time she started to make it in TV. I had just come out of a coma when she came to the hospital and leaned over my bed and whispered, "Little Mich, little Mich, don't you worry about anything. Wherever I go, I'll take care of you." And she has.

Michie Nader,
sister of Kathie Lee Gifford

When my sister made a courageous decision to go to law school at the age of fifty, leaving my mother in a house that not only had many loving teenage grandchildren in it but a kindly older woman as a paid companion besides, my mother reduced her to frequent tears by insisting that this was a family with no love in it, no home-cooked food in the refrigerator; not a real family at all.

Gloria Steinem

oooooooooooooooooooooooooooooooooooooo

The love that grew with us from our cradles never knew diminution from time or distance. Other ties were formed, but they did not supersede or weaken this. Death tore away all that was mortal and perishable, but this tie he could not sunder.

Charlotte Elizabeth Tonna

Mummy certainly feels that Margot loves her much more than I do, but she thinks that this just goes in phases! Margot has grown so sweet; she seems quite different from what she used to be, isn't nearly so catty these days and is becoming a real friend. Nor does she any longer regard me as a little kid who counts for nothing.

Anne Frank

My sister! With that thrilling word
    Let thoughts unnumbered wildly spring!
What echoes in my heart are stirred,
    While thus I touch the trembling string.

Margaret Davidson

Brenda, of course, changed her name to Crystal Gayle and is making it on her own. She used to travel around with me when she was younger, but you've got to go on your own sooner or later. Otherwise, people are always comparing you to your big sister, and nobody likes that.

Loretta Lynn

She was never dressed as a boy. She was beautiful. She made a beautiful picture, but she didn't like vaudeville. She didn't know why she should bother to learn to sing and dance, and get tired, if she didn't have to. . . . I wish my sister hadn't died at an early age. That she could have had the exquisite joy of growing old.

June Havoc,
on her sister, Gypsy Rose Lee

I cannot deny that, now I am without your company I feel not only that I am deprived of a very dear sister, but that I have lost half of myself.

Beatrice d'Este,
letter to her sister, Isabella d'Este

[She is] a bowl of golden water which brims but never overflows.

Virginia Woolf,
about her sister, Vanessa Bel

○○○○○○○○○○○○○○○○○○○○○○○○○○○○○○○○○○○○○○

For there is no friend like a sister,
In calm or stormy weather,
To cheer one on the tedious way,
To fetch one if one goes astray,
To lift one if one totters down,
To strengthen whilst one stands.

Christina Rossetti,
Goblin Market

⚜ ○ ⚜

I sought my soul,
   But my soul I could not see.
I sought my God,
   But my God eluded me.
I sought my sisters,
   And I found all three.

Anonymous

⚜ ○ ⚜

My older sister, Suzanna . . . had been sheer
perfection at birth: round, auburn-haired,
bright-eyed. I was the designated ugly duck-
ling—but more loved for all that—or so the
story went.

Erica Jong

The Gabor Sisters

I let Anne go to God, and felt He had a right to her. I could hardly let Emily go. I wanted to hold her back then, and I want her back now.

Charlotte Brontë,
on the deaths of sisters Anne and Emily

ooooooooooooooooooooooooooooooooooooooo

Two highlights of my youth revolve around
Sandy. The first: she got married when I was
six, which is *the* memory of my childhood
because one of my aunts fell through the floor
at her wedding. [The other is] when my mother
asked Sandy to pick me up at the June Taylor
School of the Dance and take me to Howard
Johnson and Radio City Music Hall, as we did
every Saturday. So Sandra, married and
divorced by now and home on vacation from
London, took me instead to the House of Chad
where we ate lobster and spare ribs and all these
things I thought were going to make me drop
dead, and then she took me to this movie called
Expresso Bongo.

Wendy Wasserstein

In thee my soul shall own combined
The sister and the friend.

Catherine Killigrew

OOO

For when three sisters love each other with such sincere affection, the one does not experience sorrow, pain, or affliction of any kind, but the others' heart wishes to relieve, and vibrates in tenderness. Like a well-organized musical instrument.

Elizabeth Shaw,
sister of Abigail Adams and Mary Cranch

꧁ ⬤ ꧂

You can't think how I depend upon you, and when you're not there the colour goes out of my life, as water from a sponge; and I merely exist, dry and dusty. This is the exact truth: but not a very beautiful illustration of my complete adoration of you; and longing to sit, even saying nothing, and look at you.

Virginia Woolf,
to Vanessa Bell

꧁ ⬤ ꧂

Liza Minelli and Lorna Luft

Geordie and Mary were able to get away with murder because if there was some upset about the house I was usually the cause of it. I was always the instigator of strange things that we did. Also, I usually took the blame because, with my dark mysterious looks, I appeared the most guilty.

Martha Graham

She's my big sister. She taught me how to ride [a motorcycle]. She didn't teach me how to stop, but she taught me how to ride.

Lee LaFurge,
about her sister, Diana Marafioti

I can see clearly, and I can think clearly; she's with me all the time. I feel like she helps me make decisions.

Denise Brown,
about her sister, Nicole Brown Simpson

When we grew up and were coming out, her favorite tease was to find out whoever it was that we fancied—which she always managed to do, whatever our efforts at secrecy—and then tell us that she had seen him at a dance the night before, where he had proposed to her. So convincing was she at this that one almost believed her, even though she did it time and time again and we knew she was teasing.

Pam Mitford,
about her sister, Nancy

My sister Jewelle was four years older than I . . . She was chatty and inquisitive, and related easily to grown-ups. She carried the confidence and assurance of the firstborn lightly on her shoulders. . . . Directing my behavior and activity became second nature to her, though generally I ignored her baton.

Shirlee Taylor Haizlip

○○

And if you do see someone with a funny hat, you must *not* point at it and laugh, and you must *not* be in too much of a hurry to get through the crowds to the tea table. That's not polite either.

Princess Elizabeth,
to her sister, Margaret

❋ ○ ❋

You should write your lonely little sister at least once a week.

Kathleen Kennedy,
to her sister, Eunice

❋ ○ ❋

Alice is the rock, the one you can call at three in the morning, and she'll always be ready to help in any way.

Reba McEntire

❋ ○ ❋

$\mathcal{M}$y most abiding memory of Lynny as a child is of the little girl who trailed behind us crying "Wait for me." Only when she too became a professional actress and had her second baby at the same time as I had my last did we transcend the gap and become close friends.

Vanessa Redgrave

The Pointer Sisters

I could go on and on about the differences between my sister and me. Despite them, we have much in common. Growing older has drawn us even closer. Jinny's a much less public person than I. She's very content with the simple things in life, and I'm not.

Kitty Dukakis

Amy was a looker; I privately thought she must be the most beautiful child on earth. She inherited our father's thick, wavy hair. Her eyes were big, and so were her lashes; her nose was delicate and fluted, her skin translucent. Her mouth curved quaintly; her lips fitted appealingly, as a cutter's bow dents and curls the water under way. Plus she was quiet. And little, and tidy, and calm, and more or less obedient.

Annie Dillard

$\mathcal{W}$e often call each other to bare our souls. Sometimes I call her to vent about issues she knows absolutely nothing about, but it's a safe environment to do that. And she does it as well.

Barbara Ross-Lee,
sister of Diana Ross

Most of the things that come up are the good-sister and evil-sister thing. I would play the evil sister.

Jennifer Tilly,
about her sister, Meg

☀ **O** ☀

How can you be a sister and not know how else you might have been? Mandy was smart, but was she smarter? I was funny, but was I funnier? I was younger. She was older. Braver. Taller. Meaner. Stronger. Sisterhood carries with it a sometimes screaming, usually silent "er," the "er" of relentless comparison.

Lisa Grunwald

☀ **O** ☀

The bond we have now is so strong, we have become my mother—together.

Diana Ross,
about her sister, Barbara Ross-Lee

☀ **O** ☀

ooooooooooooooooooooooooooooooooooooooo

Yet still my fate permits me this relief,
To write to lovely Delia all my grief.
To you alone I venture to complain;
From others hourly strive to hide my pain.

Abigail Colman Dennie,
from a letter to her sister, Jane Colman

We're getting closer together as we get older,
but there would be a slight problem of tempera-
ment. In fact, it would be bigger than
Hiroshima.

Joan Fontaine,
about her sister, Olivia de Havilland

Margaret was a genuine nuisance to me as I
self-consciously strove toward adolescence. Still,
I was glad to have a sister. I saw a lot of myself
in her from the beginning, and we would even-
tually become very close . . .

Naomi Judd

The Kennedy Sisters, with their parents

She is more silent even than I am, less gifted with the power of making friends.

Charlotte Brontë,
about her sister, Anne

* ○ *

My Own Dear Nan.

How shall I thank you for all the steps your dear feet have taken, all the hours spent in planning, all the love that kept your tender heart at work for me? I cant, & I wont try now, but it has touched me very much to find myself so loved, so anxiously cared for & remembered.

Louisa May Alcott,
to her sister, Anna, who gave her a surprise birthday party.

* ○ *

Jealousy and love are sisters.

Russian Proverb

* ○ *

An older sister helps one remain half child, half woman.

Anonymous

True sibling relationships have a varied lot of ingredients, but sympathy is rarely one of them.

Judith Martin,
Miss Manners

Dumb. Dumb. Tiny drum beats. Dumb. Dumb. Her sister's favorite word. She called her dumb more than she called her Jane.

Ann McGovern

We only argue about serious things, like if I get a stain on something and say it's not mine.

Tamera Mowry,
about her sister, Tia

The Gish Sisters

OOOOOOOOOOOOOOOOOOOOOOOOOOOOOOOOOOOOOOO

I'm envious of my sister. She's a full-time
mother.

> **Andie MacDowell**

Believe me, except Mr. Fox and my children,
there is nothing I love in this world in the least
to compare to you; . . . your happiness and
peace of mind is one of the things I have most
at heart.

> **Caroline Lennox,**
> *to her sister, Emily*

I don't know how to express my obligations to
you for such kind advice as you gave me . . .
You know, my sweet sister, how sincere I always
am in my professions of love or gratitude
towards you.

> **Louisa Lennox Connolly,**
> *to her sister, Emily*

As for Louisa, I really think that in my life I never knew or heard of anything equal to the sweetness and gentleness of her disposition. She is indeed as yet quite an angel. She is mildness itself. It is not in nature to ruffle the sweetness of her temper one single instant.

Emily Lennox

Sisters may share the same mother and father but appear to come from different families.

Anonymous

Tricia was a tomboy. And I was a girly-girl.

Joely Fisher

I put on my mom's red lipstick because I wanted to do what Heather was doing. I got it all over my face.

Nicholle Tom

I always regarded my sister as a child who I, as the older one, took care of. Even today I still call her by the diminutive "Lyudochka."

Raisa Gorbachev

Every now and then our arms would fly around each other in a hug and we'd look in each other's eyes and say how happy we were. We didn't have anything very original or profound to say. We were both so excited we were almost out of our minds; . . . We were overwhelmed at finally getting to see each other.

Berniece Baker Miracle,
sister of Marilyn Monroe

❋ ○ ❋

I knew that my sister always loved me, that she'd always take care of me. But Alline was somehow too slow and quiet for me—I was always up to something, running, moving, doing. I felt like a complete outsider, the only one of my kind. So I just went off by myself, out in the world, to walk in the pastures and be with the animals.

Tina Turner

❋ ○ ❋

The Talmadge Sisters

From the moment we were put together on this earth, we became a unit. The Mandrell Sisters. We might quarrel over a game or an item of clothing, but we never had any natural pairings, any two-against-one stuff.

Barbara Mandrell

I would take her as crew in our boat races, and I remember that she usually could do what she was told. She was especially helpful with the jib, and she loved to be in the winning boat. Winning at anything always brought a marvelous smile to her face.

Eunice Kennedy,
about her sister, Rosemary

I'd notice the beautiful faces of my two sisters—their facial bones, their very eyes. Mary was the beauty. She had blond hair and blue eyes and, even as a child, long, long legs. . . .

Martha Graham

I am very grateful to my sisters for teaching me what I know about people. For showing me different ways to grow. For never having to worry whether they'll show up for me.

Wendy Wasserstein,
on sisters Sandy and Georgette

Bessie was what we used to call a "feeling" child; she was sensitive and emotional. She was quick to anger, and very outspoken. . . . I always did what I was told. I was calm and agreeable. The way I see it, there's room in the world for both me and Bessie. We kind of balance each other out.

Sarah Louise (Sadie) Delany

❧ ○ ❧

I still loved Boud [Unity] for her huge glittering personality, for her rare brand of eccentricity, for a kind of loyalty to me which she preserved in spite of our now very real differences of outlook. When I thought about it, I had a sad and uneasy feeling that we were somehow being swept apart by a huge tidal wave over which we had no control; that from the distance a freezing shadow was approaching which would one day engulf us. Sometimes we even talked of what would happen in a revolutionary situation.

Decca Mitford,
about differences in political
views with her sister, Unity

The Bouvier Sisters

Alva, my sister, and I always called our mother Anna. All three of us were so very close to one another.

Greta Garbo

❀○❀

I don't know why, but my sisters and I thought of ballet as a familiar scenario, not a profession. The three of us shared a bedroom, and the bed was our stage. Sug was the Teacher, Beverly was the Mother, and I was the Student, Daisy.

Suzanne Farrell

❀○❀

I stood on tiptoe to look at her. She was big for a new-born child and had a wispy corona of jet-black hair so unlike the rest of us. She looked very nice sleeping peacefully and I felt suddenly happy to have a sister.

Jackie Callas,
about her sister, Maria

❀○❀

She didn't really communicate with anyone,
even her mother, except maybe God. Gloria
used to talk to God all the time. If she was having a discussion with you and she couldn't get
something across and didn't want an argument,
she would say, "I'm going to go upstairs and
talk to God"; if she couldn't share something
with you, then she knew she could share it with
God. . . . She had a relationship with the
benign forces of the universe that got her
through a lot.

> **Joy Hallward,**
> *about her sister, Gloria Grahame*

I love Eva and she loves me and if anything
happened to me she would die and if anything
happened to her I would die.

> **Zsa Zsa Gabor**

Jamie and I have run the gamut from tearing each other's hair out when we were kids, to ignoring each other, to being each other's best friend.

Kelly Curtis,
about her sister, Jamie Lee Curtis

OO

When we get to the rocking chair stage, we
plan on living in very close proximity, either side
by side or in the same house.

Dixie Carter.
about her sister, Midge

Claudia smiled sweatily and put up with all our
mishandling. She was "the baby." She knew her
place. Today she tells me how much she resented us. That was nothing to how much we
resented her merely for being born.

Erica Jong

It's miraculous to watch the breadth of her
openness.

Ashley Judd,
about her sister, Wynonna

When you're around I laugh more, and I need that because I tend to be so serious-minded. You have a way of finding humor in anything. You can pull the theater out of life. Being with you, I can be completely myself. You appreciate the stresses I have being a public figure, meeting people's expectations, fulfilling a role. When it's just us, I can be myself and know you'll love and understand me no matter what. You don't want anything from me except my happiness.

Coretta Scott King,
from a letter to her sister, Edythe

I loved being a big sister so much that I took charge automatically. I went to their classes, I organized the shows in our living room, I fussed over their clothing and their hair. I included them in whatever I was doing, not to be bossy, I liked to think, but because that was what big sisters do.

Barbara Mandrell

✦❂✦

Princess Margaret and Queen Elizabeth II

To this day I depend on my sisters for love and guidance. . . . If we don't help each other, who will?

Barbara Mandrell

❊ ○ ❊

We're best friends.

Debbie Allen,
about her sister, Phylicia Rashad

❊ ○ ❊

Anne and I say I wonder what we shall be like and what we shall be and where we shall be if all goes well, in the year 1874—in which year I shall be in my 57th year. Anne will be in her 55th year . . . and Charlotte in her 59th year. Hoping we shall all be well at that time we close our paper

Emily and Anne Brontë

❊ ○ ❊

Sisters are our peers, the voice of our times.

Elizabeth Fishel

Sisters stand between one and life's cruel circumstances.

> Nancy Mitford

＊ ○ ＊

The older daughter is married off by her parents, the younger daughter by her sister.

> Russian Proverb

＊ ○ ＊

We heard a song, we heard it in harmony.

> Maxene Andrews,
> *of the Andrew Sisters*

＊ ○ ＊

The intensity between brother and sister is likely to be less than that between two sisters because men and women occupy different spheres in relation to child rearing.

> Karen Gail Lewis

＊ ○ ＊

Nothing could ever come between us.

> Jacqueline Kennedy Onassis,
> *about her sister, Lee*